50 Words for Grief

Two Brothers' Reflections on Loss

By Daniel E. Brothers and Robert P. Brothers

ISBN: 979-8-9867432-1-9

Copyright © 2022

All Rights Reserved, No part of this book may be reproduced in any manner without express written permission of the Copyright Owner except in the case of brief quotations embodied in critical articles or reviews.

Printed and published in the USA.
Seattle, Washington

*This book is for you.
Know that I poured
love into this book,
and every ounce of it is for you.*

My older brother and I shared a great deal in common. From having an affinity for strange instruments, to our passion for understanding the natural world. Even down to our difficulty finishing projects before starting new ones. We are similar in a great many ways, but we do share our differences; the most profound of which is that Robby is no longer alive.

This will likely not come as a shock to you, either by the insinuation of the title, or by the way it was categorized by your local bookseller into the grief and loss section of the bookshop; but I can tell you that it certainly came as a shock to me.

I will forever remember the day my father found me at work in New York City. He flew overnight to tell me the horrible news. I had received a suspicious "How are you doing buddy" text from a friend hours before, and I was engrossed in the production of a K-Pop music video. I met my dad at the door surrounded by union workers moving boxes of chandeliers. His voice cracked slightly when he told me "Robby killed himself, Daniel."

I forget what I said in reply, it was hardly words, but the memory lives in slow motion and in perfect detail. I watch it like a movie every time I think of it. Me embracing my father in the doorway of a rented theater amidst the bustle of an unsleeping city. I nearly stole my boss's car keys as we fled to the airport home.

The funeral came hard and fast, with tears wetting cheeks, strange comforts from unlikely faces, and family coming together. I remember being floored by my former scoutmaster, a man I hadn't thought of much less seen since sophomore year of highschool. He singled me out, eyes cracked with loss; I don't remember what he said but I'll never forget how he said it. With determination and purpose, he shared an honest grief. Close family friends struggled to impart half of the loss he shared with me, and then he was gone.

After the whirlwind of the funeral, and a holiday season spent home and hollow. I took to the pen as my mourning drug of choice. I wrote feverishly in the winter of 2020, plays and poems and stories. Anything to get the thoughts out of my head. Anything to live somewhere other than the confines of my cubicle apartment as the pandemic hit NYC.

For a while I entertained the idea that Robby had known of the hardship 2020 would bring. Aside from the natural desire for some concrete reason he had gone, I was legitimately concerned that a zombie apocalypse was imminent. The only time suicide had ever come up in conversation between the two of us was in our differing opinions on how to react to a zombie outbreak. I personally am pro making a compound in the woods, but he always said he would rather not watch the world burn. I had the strange hope that he had known something everyone else hadn't. It wasn't until I read through his high school notebooks that I realized how long he had wrestled with depression and suicidal thought.

    I should tell you now that the idea for this book was actually his. In one of his many well worn composition books, he had collection of poems titled "50 Words for Suicide". There is a cruel and ironic part of me that wished desperately to title this book the same, but I think he would agree with me that suicide is not what this book is really about.

    Not that I do know what this book is about. II certainly don't know what Robby would say this book *is* about. I've written intros, asides, dozens of extra poems, and so much more, and I still don't know. But I do know how it starts.

    The first poem of the collection, I will confess, was penned by my own hand. But other than the last line, which I added later, I have no doubt that Robby wrote this poem through me. For the cynics out there, I know I can not prove it to you. But for those who have felt the strangeness of life when it touches death, I am telling you that I know these words are his.

When mourners were at our house before the funeral, a family friend of Hawaiian heritage looked me in the eyes, and told me that my brother would visit me in my sleep. He was calm and clear, and he spoke with the final certainty that relative strangers speak with at a funeral. I didn't know how to respond. So he emphasized, clarified, that Robby would speak to me soon in my dreams, and he would truly be there.

That night, or the next maybe, I awoke to my pen finishing the following poem. In that strange state when you can still forget where the dream ends and the day begins, I read words I had never thought.

I hope you'll be able to tell by comparison that they are his words, (his other poems are listed in the back of the book.) I will also say for the cynical, that I had not yet read any of the other works published here when I awoke to this poem. I sincerely hope you think it is his; In no small part because I do not like the way it is written. I would have put it differently, and I doubt the thought would have come to me in the first place. But I have taken pains to leave it as accurate to the initial scrawling as I can.

Whatever it is, it's a start. Hopefully by the end, we might know what this book is about. Thank you for your indulgence, and please tell someone you love that you love them.

I Wonder

I wonder what made the stars
all come to rest where they are.
Not literally,
I mean,
they're not really resting.

They're moving rather rapidly
and so are we.
But I do wonder

What would life have been like
millions of years ago?
What did the dinosaurs really act like?
Birds?
All of it!
We've lost so much,
and confused so much else,
of the fossil record.

I wonder what would have happened If I had called,
with a belt in my hand,
my phone in the other.
Who would have picked up?
In the dark,
lost,
Like so many bones in the ground,
so many stars in the sky.

I wonder what Christmas will be like next year.

Eulogy

I thought I'd start by sharing a few things about Robby that I have learned and have been reminded of this week.

There is a crayon drawing to prove that he was ahead of the whole climate change thing from a young age, if he were president that would have been his top priority. He would carry a rock in his pocket sometimes, most of the times. He was a talented writer, with poems more bittersweet in his passing. He had an especially good impression of a British policeman. As he was running, his face went from "I might actually like this" to "oh god why am I doing this". He once wrote and played a song with only one hand.

When asked who his friends were, he made a spreadsheet. On that topic, you'd be hard pressed to find a better boyfriend who planned his relationships on excel.

I worry, like many of us do, "what could I have done" or "what did I do"? What of my actions helped him or hurt him in some way, in some wonderful way, in some terrible way? And I am sure that sometimes what we did hurt, and other times it helped. I'm of the unpopular opinion that you should remember both.

Robby was a sad person for most of his life. He was often downtrodden. I remember leaving him out, stealing his jokes, and laughing at his expense with his friends. It's important to remember these things. Because within all of that and throughout all of that. Throughout the negativity perceived and also given, and the difficult path he tread.

Robby was a happy person. He was a kind and caring ear and hand to so many people, including myself. He was gentle and loving in a way only dogs could understand. He would forgive everyone time and again because he had faith in people, in persons. Trust was a given for him. And that was true despite the times that you were mean to him, or pushed him off, or said you would listen to his podcast or song or whatever.

He wasn't kind when it was convenient or easy, he was kind. He was. He was happy, and he was sad. He was kind and beautiful, <u>and</u> he is dead. Remember what he is doesn't sully what he was, and what he was does not negate what he is. Remember both, the good and the bad, the alive and the dead. To forget either would be to stray from the truth, and the truth is what we seek, is who we are.

I do not know if he has found the truth after death, but I will leave you with his words so that you know that he sought to find the truth when he lived…

If I Fail To See

If I fail to see where I'm going. If I fail to see what I'm writing. If I fail to see who I am.

I hope you can forgive me.

If I stumble. If I make unfulfilled promises. If I leave unachieved goals scattered throughout my life.

I hope you can understand, it is not meant as disrespect, it is not a lack of passion.

If I am silent. If I am sullen. If I am unproductive.

I hope you can find it in yourself to love me anyway.

Because if I fail to see myself through all my fear and insecurity,

as I dig my way out through all of my dreams and other dead things,

I hope I can find your hand,

waiting there to pull.

If I fail to see.

The News.

I always cry at the laundromat.
The news is playing,
and I never watch the news.

When your world was collapsing,
or when it fell,
or when I felt it break.
There was no story on the news for you.

In a way I am grateful you're not a hashtag,
but a note would have been nice.

Pressure

Has anyone told people
that the windows on airplanes
are not screens,
and that they truly hurtle
fast above the clouds?

I think airlines enjoy the illusion of
not that.
But it is so!

And everytime I hold my nose
to pop my ears
and relieve the pressure,
I don't think of the deep blue ocean
full of life where I learned the trick.

I think of when you told me
you'd never do that,
because if you did it once
you could never go back
to doing it the natural way,
by yawning or whatever.

I hope the irony is not lost on you.

Crooked

There is a painting on my wall
that is a little crooked.

It's been like that for a while.

But every time I look at it,
what's the opposite of a smile?

I'm deflecting, the painting is crooked.

It has been for a long time.

Change it, I'll say.

I need a hammer, I'll say.

It kind of works like it is,

I'll say.

And it still stays crooked, it still stays off kilter.

I'm not sure if it doesn't feel right to straighten it.

I'm not sure if I'm happy enough to let it be.

But there is a wall behind my painting,
and it's looking a little crooked.

Ghosts

I keep my ghosts in a drawer at my desk
under piles of trash I call work.
I could get rid of them,
but I don't.
Exhuming them feels wrong,
But I won't walk on the grave.

I don't work anymore.
Instead I say my desk is haunted,
by the ghosts in my head.
and what good are ghosts,
that are never read?

The Met

You never went to central park,
to walk the path
that winds the hill
behind The Met museum.

To see the rocks
that break the ground there.

I want to ask you what kind of rock it is.
I think I know the answer,
but I don't know for sure.

Would they let you back just to take a quick peak?
Just to stand on the hill where I can't see you,
and you could spy through a glass,
or a crystal ball.

You could ID the rock.
Since you used to know them all.
And I could wait on the path,
that winds the hill
behind The Met museum.

And you could shout the name to me,
and I could hear you once again.

Resting

My mind has been sleeping as my body has worked,

moving things with my hands as dark thoughts have lurked.

By no means forgotten and by no other means lost,

my thoughts have been sleeping, I wonder the cost.

Storm

The storm reminds me of you.
Not for its rage or its bluster.
Not for its lightning nor its thunder.
Not even for the patter of rain
on the metal roof at night.

You never learned to dance in the rain;
defeated by clouds when
your eyes were full of stars,
plucking drops on your guitar.

The storm reminds me of you
Being stuck in your head with no one but you.

Leaves

A tree is a tree without its leaves,

but leaves only exist as context.

The problem is that we're taught,

The leaves of the tree,

but not the tree itself.

"This is a Maple, this is an Oak."

That is not a Maple, or an Oak, or an Ash, or a Chestnut,

That's what they wear.

A Dead Branch

A tree grows with a rotten branch
by a lake with a calming breeze.

And though it holds this great dead weight
it stands with relative ease.

Decaying wood by new spring buds
might seem a detriment,

why not cleanse the scar of death,
why cling to what's been spent?

Perhaps it waits for a wind most strong
to prune with a powerful gust.

The limb which then, will meet the ground
and moss will grow like rust.

But till that day, the tree will grow
and shade its scar with leaves.

A dead branch, or a sentiment?
Such is the way of trees.

A Lean-To

There is a lean-to at the end of my favorite hike,
and it's certainly not the only lean-to, nor my only favorite hike,
but I know that it's there.

No matter how long I'm away from the wilderness,
from the rapids rushing over rocks, mixing the scent of pine
with dark brown algae and earth,
I know that it's still there.

Simple, as most lean-to's are, great old trees and rocks
turned into a safe spot to rest, and hide from the flies.
I know what it's like to rest there.

I can visit it in my brain, though I'm usually far away.
The distance almost makes it easier to recall,
in a strange way.

So distant it becomes a constant,
stationary in my mind, and sweeter for it.
Because I left the flies behind, and took the pine and the earth,
and the rocks are there too.

What would I do if one day I walked down the path
and found an empty clearing? No note, no smoke.
Just an empty clearing where rapids rush and breed flies

in hard rocky pools.

Would I sit on the rocky earth where once was shade,
deer flies buzzing for blood about my head?
Would I tell myself, "Nothing is stationary in the planetary sense."
As I hurdle wildly around the sun?

I mean it is only natural for a lean-to to go away,
structures are only temporary after all.
Only natural,
that it too would scent the air with rotting pine,

But what would I do when I left that clearing
At the end of my favorite hike?
How would I rectify a lifetime worth of hikes,
thousands of happy rests in the shade,
with a harsh barren reality?

As I turn the bend, just over the fallen log,
to see an empty clearing where a lean-to once was;
my salt sweat tears mix with the scent of pine,
dark green algae, and dirt.

I find a bare, hot rock, dappled with leaves
Already filling the space where the lean-to once was.
I sit, to find a new constant for the end of my favorite hike.
Hot, and swarmed by deer flies out for blood.

Confession

I worry I'll have to die for my poems to be good.
That my doodles will become my life's work,
is a horror.

That alone
could keep me alive.

If only the same were true for you,
whose life's work was left before draft two.

Ceiling

I want to walk on my ceiling,

always free of my cluttered life.

No dirt on its surface.

I brush the cobwebs religiously,

like sweeping the snakes out of Ireland,

so at least one place in my tattered room is pure.

Dreamer

I used to be a dreamer.
How bleak, it's not so bad.
I still dream sometimes.
But I used to be a dreamer.

My days spent in the sun
My feet on the ground
My body under trees
My eyes in the clouds

When I was a dreamer
I dreamt of bright futures,
Of what I'd buy with a million dollars,
Of what I'd do if I could stop time,
Of what it would be like to fly!
Through pear shaped clouds
That steal my gaze from school work
Or work, work.

That steal me from all the things I dreamed
I was doing.

It's not sad that I'm no longer a dreamer.

Because I live the life I dreamed of,
In a city where the trains roll by my window,
With thousands of interesting people on them.

People I could meet one day,
could get to know,
could fall in love…
The dreams are still in me.

The dreamer is not.

Because as I lie under this tree
With my body in the dirt,
And I look up at a cloudless sky.
Every dream a dreamer could dream up
circles back,
like a vulture,
to what would you say if you could visit me on my balcony, and
watch the trains go by
full of all the people you're not.

I used to be a dreamer
And I have made my peace with that

Myself

I sleep my days away, filling my head with constant noise.
Podcasts, music, the endless feed of videos,
The fan stays on to put me to sleep.
Drowning out dreams.
I am not 'most myself' when I am with you anymore,
I'm just myself.
And though last night I slept in the arms of a woman I love,
This morning I am alone.

The Darkness in the Deep

Across the world, a steady rain of silt, clay, and dead algae settles in slow motion towards the bottom of the sea. It does not do so quickly. Occasionally something larger than algae falls from the ocean overhead, a dead fish or bird which survived the gauntlet of scavengers living in the miles of water overhead.

This is rare. The open ocean is populated only sparsely with organisms, and the probability of one dying in a position to disturb any specific patch of mud is absurd. So the bottom of the ocean is a quiet place. And a dark place. Light has a difficult time reaching too far into the depths of the ocean. Were you to descend from the surface and follow the raining microscopic organisms to their final resting place, you would quickly run out of light and face a miles-long stretch of darkness between you and journey's end.

If a dust storm is a deluge, the rain of mud in the ocean is a sunny afternoon. The sediments collect unbearably slowly in some parts of the ocean. When your feet touch the muddy ooze on the bottom, you've already displaced all of the sediment that accumulated in human history, and then some. A large scoop of your hand could remove all of the sediment since the human species evolved. But even at this monumentally slow rate of deposition, you'd have to dig a hole as deep as a 20-story building is high, to find the ash layer left by the dinosaur-killing asteroid.

Find the oldest piece of ocean on Earth. Find a piece of ocean as old as our planet. There is no such place, but imagine one. Imagine a quiet piece of ocean sitting undisturbed since the formation of the planet four and a half billion years ago. Imagine, once more, that this impossibly old piece of ocean is where you landed. That is where your footprint has removed civilization and your hand, the human species. You stand at the mouth of your 20-story hole in the ocean floor and stare at the bottom, at the year the triceratops died and you wonder, how deep is this mud? So you dig. You've been doing it for awhile already, although there's no way to tell exactly how long.

The human concept of time does not apply to this place, where the second hand is ticked at the millennia. There is no concept of a year here, not even a day. The darkness never changes, it doesn't ebb and flow with the coming and going of the seasons. A season is simply too short a time to be remembered in the mud. Four thousand seasons fight to add a millimeter of dust to the ocean floor, the voice of any individual lost in the din of millennia.

As you reach, finally, the bottom of your new trench, a fine veneer of mud covers your back, and you find yourself at the bottom of a hole some four kilometers deep, some one thousand three hundred stories deeper than the hole you dug to see the dinosaur killer. The Grand Canyon fits in your hole twice, with enough leftover room for The Empire State Building on top.

The new abyss is deep, and dark, but no darker and no less timeless than the ocean floor four kilometers above. The second hand waits, expectantly, as the first few grains of dust settle from the ocean above.

Former Catholic

The scar appeared on my wrist,
I did not put it there.
That's what I told myself.
Frantic with worry as my
woodworker hands
wrung themselves on a crowded train.

It just happened to me, a bump
a scratch.
I just hadn't noticed something sharp,
yet the mystery haunts me.

I know the only thing between me
and myself
is a thin veil of discipline.
So easily popped by a single blade
as thin as a hair.
What is more frightening is
All that keeps the balloon full is faith.

The Tree on the Point of the Bay

The sun sets, almost finding
the second crook in the mountains
that overlook the vast blue body of the lake.
Boundless, though all of its bounds are in sight,
Nearly.

Boats race into view from behind
the tree on the point of the bay,
the evergreen that keeps dark blue ripples
secreted away in the hidden waters beyond.

The tree has stood there as long as I've been alive,
longer.
And even though I have been past its point
and seen the great blue waters,
and the deep green horizon,
and the houses hidden beyond;
I loathe to think that it would fall before I do.

I dream that it would not fall at all,
that it would grow sentinel on the point of the bay,

dwarf the mountains as they crumbled,
foster a new forest of trees.

I dream that my nephews nephew,
his grandchildren,
the daughters and sons of my family
for until we are no more,
could float and see the perfect green pine and wonder.

How deep are the waters beyond?
How far do the waves stretch?
How fast do the boats race?
Just beyond,

the tree at the point of the bay.

I cry to think that it would fall before I do.
That a coffin for me made of it's timbers
could bury me with it.
That I could drift beyond the veil,
in a ship of its body.
Revealing its mysteries
and hiding mine forever.

The sun has set on the tree and me
as I float on a dock in its bay.
And though I am not a praying man
in darkness I will say,
if god is real and can hear my plea
I hope he'll answer me.
If that tree should fall deep in the night
I pray instead take me.

Cracks

I used to step
on cracks in the sidewalk,
because I thought it was
so illogical to think
 it could break your mother's back.

How could a crack even?
Even metaphorically!
Preposterous.

But I don't step on cracks anymore,
or watch TV.
I wear green on saint patrick's day,
and don't pick up pennies with their heads down.

Because now that I know the impossible,
the illogical!
That's just what happens sometimes.

Boogieman

I miss being afraid of the dark,
of dark forests, and long armed monsters.
Of things with claws pulling at the foot of my bed.

Wendigos, and Chupacabras,
Bigfoots and Yetis.

Demons, Devils, Fiends.

I make pentagrams in vain hope.
Shout Bloody Mary in the mirror,
I want these things to be true.

Because if the boogieman is in the closet,
and the trees are full of fey,
then maybe, just maybe,
We'll meet again one day.

Waiting

When?

Will I know when?

Has it already passed?

I can imagine hearing you again.
Intrusive as I wait.

Hours left
By my count.

I'll be the oldest brother
No longer the middle child.

I hold my wrists in trepidation.
The responsibility weighs on me. Like
 the ticking clock,
when you lie awake waiting for the alarm to ring.

24

I left a steady plane for worlds of uncertainty.
   I miss the sureness of my feet, but god…
      …what wonders there are to see.

25

The ground is solid on my boots,
Laced solidly for the long walk.
My belt, one hole tighter for the weight I've lost.
My back, one knot tighter for the weight I've gained.
My heart, no lighter for the peace I've found.

I set out into unfamiliar territory,
leaving my peace in pieces behind me,
to find my truth the long way round.

After

Is your time still rolling forward?
Or is it going backwards?
Are you a year younger now?
Do your birthdays, six feet under bring you closer to the start?
Not that I could say where that is exactly,
I can't even say now that you're 26, or 25, or 27!
It pains me to think how I don't know if I care anymore.

Not that I do not miss you,
and weep for you in bed.
Not that those hard set thoughts
don't live inside my head.
It no longer truly matters if you're 24 or 25,
the year is inconsequential when you're no longer alive.

Winter

The winter trees seem dead to me
but then I'm not a tree.
To garden is not my state of being,
I don't grow leaves for free.
I wish that every spring I could
push life out of my bark,
or if not that, at least provide
a home for passing lark.
But I cannot, nor can I stand
seeing mottled shafts of gray.
Standing tall and lifeless
on a beautiful sunny day
So if a tree can take advice,
or even hear my plea.
I'll tell the spring to hurry up,
if you just grow some leaves.

Ink

I sleep on ink stained sheets,
With the lights on.
Trying to illuminate
A dark mind.

Overexpose the black spots.
So it's all lost in the white light,
As encompassing as shadow
And as hopeful as new love.

Never tell me to buy new bedding,
You might as well say never to dream again.

Comfortable

Two years
of comfortable loss,
resting heavy
on my weighted blanket.
Peaceful,
subdued,
alone.
Where to go anyway?

Unsaid

I write bad poems,

but they are usually written.

Not hidden in my pen.

Not broken on my phone.

Notes, unsent texts,

things left unsaid,

at least in a poem it's not in my head.

Visit

Are you there?

In the pale glow of light behind the building,
kissing the line where brick meets sky,

Is that you?

Do you cling to the edge?
Or paint it with your presence?

If it is you,
In the light of a city bright night,
watching me write on my balcony,

Could you speak up?

All I hear is the rumble of the train in the tunnel,
And the drops of water on my glass.

Space

You sat in the window seat,
when you left for the city that killed you.
Did you look out as it landed and know?
Or did you look back east, at the home you left behind?

No, I know you.
You spent the whole flight looking at the line where the stars meet the air,
into that endless expanse.

You never landed I don't think.
You stayed locked in the thin air as the plane took your body away
and the earth took your life away
as it orbited through space leaving you drifting in the void.

I'm a frequent flier now, hoping to catch a flight that intersects with the point in space where the plane left you. You aren't here to tell me that our orbit is shifting, and that the galaxy is constantly moving to new territory in space.

That we are millions of miles removed from your spot in the universe. That the plane will never intersect that point again.

But everytime I fly, I will stare at the pale blue line and hope, at least until we get close enough for you to tell me yourself that you're gone.

Breath

She sat in the doorway
Oxygen Tank on the floor
Abandoned
Tossed like a can of pop
All for a lie
Her heart told her
"The air is real outside"
Crisp and cool
Laced with citrus
Like Fanta
Filling her lungs
That could take no more
Abandoning life stretching canisters
To accept the cool embrace of suffocation
A gift
To at least smell the lilac on the breeze
And not to die to the acrid smell
Of metal in plastic tubes

Hardwood floors scattered
With fresh cut grass and flowers
Feeling soft underfoot.

Alone

I wish I were there now,
to gently loosen the belt on your neck.

And hold you close
like we never did,
for fear of some falsehood.

And let you know
that you're my brother
and my truest love.

I would take the belt from you,
and ask you eye to eye,
If you wanted me to.

And I would kill you myself.

I would kill you myself,
so I could sleep
and know.

You didn't die alone.

So you could look in the eyes
of what killed you.

So that no one would believe
it was yourself.

Because it wasn't.

Snow

I woke up to see melted snow
after I watched it fall.
I wonder why it had to go
or if it fell at all.
Boot Prints left in frosted grass,
lost in sunlight's silent mass.
Asking broken blades to grow,
and answer to the summer's call.

Necromancy

I feel spring on my skin.
I breathe wet air
through dry lungs,
who forgot the relief
of breathing deep in
the dank bedroom of winter.

Sirens fill the sky,
as we all come alive.

The ghosts are stirring
in the warm air.
Creaking, cracking bones,
sprouting green skin in fat boils
that fill the air with fragrance.

The smell of rain in the park,
bringing the catacombs to life.

Darkness

The encroaching darkness
of a springtime forest.

Leaves filling empty space,
where moonlight once played
on the knobby knuckles of
gray white trees.

Blotting out the stars with life,
leaving live leaves.

Oh violent spring!

Throwing the glade into shadow
casting shade with green.

Hallowed in the light of the moon in May,
oh would it be any other way?

Dictionary

I didn't realize then
why I hated words.
Why each letter spelled
a different word for pain.
And each sentence
a steel trap.

But as I step off the ground over
dark waters,
and walk weightless through the air,
hand in hand with a love
who kisses beautiful words into my back;
I am embittered by
the winter nights I thought were warm
before I met the sun.

Sliver

I prefer to be trusting.

I freely give some trust to all people, and more to those I let close.

Only when that trust is broken do I stop to think if it's deserved.

I pick up the broken pieces of trust like shards of glass, the edges cutting into my palm and slivers working their way into my heart. I fashion the parts back into a whole, and if I see no ill intent, I once again give the one who broke it my trust.

Cracked.

Fragile.

But mendable.

Only when my heart
is so full of slivers
that my blood is choked
and I cannot fit
the broken pieces together
will I leave them on the floor.

(W)hole

I've got a trick for you.

I can stand completely still
while moving a hundred miles an hour.

I won't hold you back,
because i know how it feels
to be your own roadblock.

I have fought to bridge the sea of apathy
we are standing on the shore of.

Confronted with the gates of hell
I turn to say
It was worth it
I was beautiful.

And I would give my soul to write a song
the shape of the hole in my chest.

Mapmaker

You are hidden
In the depths,
and I could delve my
life away to find you.
In the streams of data,
numbers fill a cavernous underdark.
But I don't need eyes to see.
I bump my feet into
stalagmites and file folders,
I can feel my way.
Warmed rock reminds me the path,
to a den we made in our minds alone.
Unreal until it's found,
If ever we can wake from slumber.
Sleepwalking in the dark,
Dreaming maps across the gap.

Mirror

Im worried you may be real,
and that to love you
would not be an escape from myself,
a solace in sex,
an addiction to feeling.

No sprinting into the arms of a lover
embraced in the warmth,
and ignoring what I ran from.

I'm worried you'll be transparent, and reflective.

That I'll see through you the things I ran from,
that I'll see in you the man I have become.
Despite my failures.

What a burden you carry on my back.
To be to me the things I think I lack.

A Shame

I forgot what love is,
A dangerous ill, but common,
Though few souls admit it.

It's blessed to be around,
Becomes like the air,
Saturated like humidity.

It can feel a nuisance in excess
But in absence?

In absence I remember what it means.
To hear a voice on Mondays
To fantasize our some days
To plot out our one days.

In absence every moment feels
A moment wasted.

Each poem a failure
Grasping at what was never there
In hopes that something that never was
Will be.

For I forgot what love was,
And my brother, so did he.

A note

Have you ever met the girl of your dreams?

Hi, I'm Robby. I use he/him pronouns and a while back, I had a dream.

I remember exactly three things about this dream, 1 the sun was setting, 2 at some point, and I'm not sure for how long, there was a castle, and 3 I met the most stunning, fantastic, beautiful, perfect girl.

I don't remember what she looked like, but in that dream I felt whole, I felt complete,
I felt happy.

Not just the I-found-money-in-my-pocket happy or mom-made-my-favorite meal happy, or any of those other families of happy, but the ecstatic joy that only happens when you know everything is right and proper and good in your tiny corner of the universe. In this state I drifted slowly, and I dare say even gracefully to consciousness. I opened my eyes, looked to my side, and she was gone. Worse. She was never there.

Many things went through my head. Confusion, Sadness, Anger, but mostly, and overpoweringly
Desperation.
I begged, pleaded, with god and the universe and whoever else was listening, I wanted her, needed her back. I paced and ran and screamed. GIVE HER BACK. Give her back.

Perfect

I wish I knew your name,
or what your face looked like in the moonlight.
I wish I could call you now and every single night.

But I don't know you.
You haven't met me and I haven't met you.
All I can do is sit here, and pray that you exist
outside of my head.

Close

It's close

Im close to hundreds

Tumbling through the dryer

Warm, softened and clean smelling

Taking the wetness from our tears and

Wicking it away

Burning candles and looking

In lovers eyes to avoid the clutter building under the rug

I'm falling still

I'm writing still

The end is fast approaching

The back cover flipping closer

The ground rushing to meet me

But you aren't buried in the ground

The air took you from me

No trees root in you to make new paper for my pen.

I can't stop the tumble

Any way but one

And since the air is full of you

I think I'll breathe deeply.

A Note for the Following Poem

As best as I can tell, barring shorthand notes and grocery lists, the following are my brother's last written words.

11/25/2019

There is something about a café
with a perfect taste in music.

Fear

It is too broad,
when people say they fear the unknown.
It is also untrue.
Things truly unknown, we are ignorant of,
we cannot fear
even if we should.

What is terrifying is the known,
the perceived.
The shadow of a figure,
the sound in the woods,
the death of a friend.

And while the shadow is really a coat on the wall,
and the sound is just a squirrel.
The death is just that.

It takes no explanation.
It needs no reasoning.
In a way, there is no unknown in it.
They were, and now they aren't.
The unknown is in the question.

When will I die?
And How?
And what happens after?
The fear is in the knowledge that the only ones
who can answer those questions,
can not,
until you know as well

Calm

There is a moment you realize
that the water has calmed down.
You've watched it bluster
for hours and hours
and not noticed a change.
But as the sunlight shifts
like a dream in a movie,
and you happen to watch
the flag float gently down.
You realize that the lake at least,
is calm.
And the cool air tastes delicious!

Nightfall

In the dark of the setting sun
I catch the last glimpse
of the tree on the point of the bay.
My eyes strain to make its shape out,
against the green dark mountains beyond.

Despite my prayers, my desires
my wonder,
I know this is my last look at the pine.
This year, at least.

But the world is big, and the lake is small.
Finite, despite what the tree makes it seem.

It is only natural to leave it be,
only human to keep it afar,
to wish it well in my absence.

And though I doubt this will be my last time,
I know it could be,
Which is a strange comfort to me.

The mountain's shadows stretch
o'er the tree and me
as I leave its peaceful bay.
And for what good a prayer is,
I feel obliged to say.
God if you're real and you can hear,
I hope you'll think of me.
As I walk off into the night,
and sun sets on the tree.

About the Author

Robby Brothers (1994-2019) was a writer, researcher, and musician who took his own life after a lifelong struggle with depression. He was 25 years old.

He was most at home at the top of a very tall mountain, or lost in the deep woods of the adirondacks. His passion for the natural world and good science pervaded all of his work. His scholarly passions were paleontology, astronomy, and geology.

He was a talented cello and mandolin player, and you can hear his original music on the youtube channel Last Name Brothers.

About the Author

Daniel Brothers(1996-Present) is a NYC based writer, playwright, and props maker.

His first foray into publishing and poetry has been rewarding and taxing, his future projects include "Living Together" a new play, and a fantasy novel set in the Adirondacks.

He has been known to take his tortoise out for walks in prospect park, and is currently learning how to play the accordion.

For more up to date info on his exploits in theater and literature see: dannyjbrothers.com

Poems and Prose by Robby Brothers

Pg 7   I Wonder
Pg 11 If I Fail to See
Pg 19 Leaves
Pg 28 The Darkness in the Deep
Pg 38 24
Pg 53 Sliver
Pg 54 (W)hole
Pg 58 A Note
Pg 59 Perfect
Pg 62 11/25/2019

Made in the USA
Middletown, DE
17 April 2023